ART SOUVENIR

... OF ...

REPRESENTATIVE MEN,
PUBLIC BUILDINGS,
PRIVATE RESIDENCES,
BUSINESS HOUSES,
AND POINTS OF INTEREST

... IN ...

TERRE HAUTE, IND.

PREPARED FOR THE

TERRE HAUTE GAZETTE.

1894.

KELLY BROTHERS, PUBLISHERS.

THE Gazette's object in the publication of this volume is to give a pictorial representation of Terre Haute's citizens, institutions and points of interest as they appear in 1894. Pictures, and especially those made from the ever minutely accurate camera, convey impressions much more clearly than words. For this reason the descriptive matter which prefaces the photographs is much condensed and is chiefly statistical. Some of the photographs are old, but most of them have been taken especially for this volume and are, therefore, up to date. The idea has been to make a book so convenient in size, so excellent in printing and so durable in binding that it will not be put away in some drawer to be mislaid, but will be entitled to a position on the center table with the family photographs.

Of course it is not complete. It has been impossible to get some photographs which ought to be in it; but it is thoroughly representative of the professional and business men of the city.

Such a pictorial history will have increasing interest as the years roll by. A similar volume ought to be issued every five or ten years.

HISTORICAL.

Terre Haute and Indiana are of the same age. Both were born in 1816.

In the great territory between the Mississippi river and the Allegheny mountains and the lakes and the Ohio river, the Wabash is the most considerable river. On the east bank of the stream, midway between its head waters and its mouth, nature had placed an elevated plateau. It was the natural site for a town. The highland that made it the proper location for a town suggested to the French voyageurs its name of Terre Haute.

Later on the descriptive appellation of the Prairie City was given it, when the little cluster of houses huddled together on the river bank had spread out from the thin fringe of forest skirting the river at that point to the open prairie beyond. But tree planting along the streets and in the yards began so early, and was prosecuted so persistently, that Forest City would be more appropriate than Prairie City now.

Terre Haute is in latitude 39° 28′ north, longitude 10° 20′ west. Its altitude above sea level is 498 feet.

One Joseph Kitchell had entered the land on which the town stands, acquiring title from the government. Of him it was purchased by the Terre Haute Land Company consisting of Cuthbert and Thomas Bullitt, of Louisville, Abraham Markle, Hyacinth La Salle and Jonathan Lindley. They organized a town company and filed the original town plat October 25th, 1816, and an amended plat May 20th, 1825. When it became incumbent upon the three commissioners appointed by act of the legislature to locate a county seat for the newly organized county of Vigo, the Terre Haute Town Company secured it by a donation of the public square and other lots, and $4,000 for the erection of a court house and other buildings.

The first census of the town was taken by the late Charles T. Noble in 1829, for his own satisfaction, and showed 579 inhabitants. Another census was taken by Mr. Noble, August 5th, 1835, and it disclosed a population of 1,214 inhabitants. The United States census of 1840 showed 2,300; 1850, 3,572: 1860, 8,594; 1870, 16,103; 1880, 26,042; 1890, 30,217.

Incorporation as a town was accomplished under act of the legislature Jan. 26th, 1832. April 30th, 1843, it was decided by a popular vote to become a city and the first election for city officers occurred on the 30th of May, 1843, the total number of votes cast at the election being 752.

In its early days the only way of getting to Terre Haute or away from it was by the river. Other towns were far distant. Man set to work to bring them near. The first step was the completion, in 1823, as far as Terre Haute, of the National Road, that great highway projected from Maryland to Missouri by the national government. In 1849 the Wabash and Erie Canal was opened and the first boat reached the town. It was an epoch in its history. But the canal was doomed almost before it was done, for in 1852 the railroad from Terre Haute to Indianapolis was opened and the frontier town of a few years before was thenceforth to be linked by iron bands to all the continent. Other roads followed in quick succession until today it is the center of nine roads radiating from it as the spokes from the hub of a wheel, making it as a railroad center the second city in Indiana.

In certain widely divergent lines Terre Haute stands pre-eminent among her sister cities of the State. No other city of Indiana has so many educational institutions or so many students. She is the Athens and Alexandria of Indiana.

In the production of pig iron and the manufactures into which iron enters, no other city in the State approaches Terre Haute. This is also true of the manufactured products from corn, and of the production of alcohol.

In those essential elements of urban existence, light, water, cheap fuel gas and street transportation, she is equipped as well as any city in world, for she has the latest and best.

Within the next few years there is every reason to expect a development and a growth greater than at any time in the past, for her advantages are every day becoming better known and all they need, to be appreciated, is to be known.

EDUCATIONAL ADVANTAGES.

Terre Haute is the educational center of Indiana. This is not an idle boast; it is a fortunate fact. There are other cities which have important educational institutions. Lafayette, Greencastle and Bloomington all have one college each, of which the citizens of the State may be justly proud; but Terre Haute has a number, and among them the largest State institution—The Indiana State Normal, with an attendance of 1,200; the Rose Polytechnic Institute; two Female Colleges; two Commercial Colleges, and a great free and parochial school system. Education of both sexes in all branches may be here obtained. The advantages are so obvious as to attract the attention of parents all over the country. The following is a brief review of the schools:

ROSE POLYTECHNIC.

Owing to the munificence of the late Chauncey Rose, Terre Haute can boast of as fine a school as there is in the country, in the Rose Polytechnic Institute, which is devoted to higher education of young men in chemistry, mechanical, civil and electrical engineering.

It was incorporated in 1874 under the name of Terre Haute School of Industrial Science. The corner stone of the "academic building" was laid on the 11th of September, 1875, and on the same day the board of managers amended the articles of incorporation, changing the name of the association to the "Rose Polytechnic Institute."

The Institute was opened March 7th, 1883. The following persons compose the board of managers:

Hon. Richard W. Thompson, LL. D., - - President.
Ray G. Jenckes, Esq., - - - - - - Secretary.
Demas Deming, Esq., - - - - - - Treasurer.

Hon. William Mack, Preston Hussey, Esq., Wm. C. Ball, A. M.
Leslie D. Thomas, A. M., William S. Rea, Esq., Robert S. Cox, M E.

PUBLIC SCHOOLS.

The Terre Haute free public school system dates from January 21st, 1853. Sixty-three different persons, twenty-five of whom are still living, have served in the capacity of school trustees. James Hook is the sole survivor of the first school board. The life of the late Miss Jane Hersey was closely related to the history of our schools, she having taught in Terre Haute's public schools from 1853 to 1892.

The growth of the schools is not in any way more clearly manifested, perhaps, than in the obligations of the treasurer of the board. In 1853 the bond was $3,000; it is now $200,000.

LIST OF SUPERINTENDENTS.

Wm. M. Ross, - - Sept. 9, 1853, to July 14, 1854.
James H. Moore, - Sept. 5, 1860, to Mar. 17, 1862.
Joseph W. Snow, - - Sept. 1, 1862, to Sept. 1, 1863.
John M. Olcott, - Aug. 17, 1863, to Sept. 4, 1869.
Wm. H. Wiley, - - June 3, 1869, to present time.

PUBLIC SCHOOL BUILDINGS.

DISTRICTS.	LOCATIONS.	VALUES
High School	Seventh and Walnut	$ 85.000
First	Fourth and Mulberry	34.000
Second	Seventh and Swan	24.500
Third	Third and Farrington	25.500
Fourth	635 North Fifth	18.000
Fifth	Twelfth and Chestnut	24.500
Sixth	Twelfth and Ohio	40.500
Seventh	1421 Second Ave	24.000
Eighth	17th St. and Franklin Ave	7.500
Ninth	Third and Oak	5.700
Tenth	1500 South 13½	4.500
Eleventh	In Normal	.400
Twelfth	Second and Crawford	6.000
Thirteenth	Third St. and 8th Ave	.700
Fourteenth	Sixteenth and Elm	5.000
Fifteenth	Eighteenth and Chestnut	2.500
Sixteenth	Eighth and College	25,000
Seventeenth	Seventh St. and Third Ave	27.000
Public Library	709½ Wabash Ave	11.000
Office	In High School	.300
Total		$ 371.600

The enrollment during 1894 was 5,976.

THE TERRE HAUTE PUBLIC LIBRARY.

709½ Wabash Avenue, Mrs Lucy C. Wonner, Librarian. Contains 10,583 volumes. It is under the direction and control of the Board of School Trustees.

THE INDIANA STATE NORMAL.

The act of the General Assembly which erected the Indiana State Normal School was approved December 20, 1865. Terre Haute gave the ground and $50,000 in cash. The school opened January 6, 1870. The building was destroyed by fire, April 9, 1888. The accumulation of eighteen years was destroyed. The city provided suitable temporary quarters and subscribed $50,000 to rebuild the school. The State gave $100,000 and the building was rebuilt by Shewmacker and Junclaus, of Indianapolis. In 1892 the legislature gave $40,000 for an additional building. The attendance this year (1894) was over 1,200. Total number of students since the opening has been 10,220.

The Summer School is now a permanent and vabuable feature of the Normal, and is conducted with much ability.

TERRE HAUTE COMMERCIAL COLLEGE.

The Terre Haute Commercial College was founded in 1862, by Prof. William H. Garvin, and is one of the great schools of the State. There are about 250 students in the four departments of shorthand, typewriting, actual business and telegraphy. All the branches usually taught in the best commercial schools are included in the course. The faculty consists of seven teachers. It is now conducted by Prof. W. C. Isbell.

GARVIN COMMERCIAL COLLEGE.

Garvin's Commercial College was opened the first part of the year 1893, by a stock company, composed of business men of Terre Haute. It is located at the north east corner of Third and Wabash Avenue. The course of study includes book-keeping, penmanship, commercial law, business forms, shorthand and typewriting. The enrollment numbers about thirty-five pupils. The school is now owned and conducted by Messrs Will Garvin and Patrick W. Haggerty.

COATES COLLEGE.

Coates College is a plant of the Presbyterian Church, under the care of the General Assembly's Board of Aid for Colleges. and was founded March 17, 1885, by Mrs. Jane Patterson Coates, of Greencastle.

Coates College is situated on a plateau at the foot of Sixth Street, on what is known as the "Strawberry Hill." The grounds abound in wild flowers and forest trees.

The school and grounds occupy 13 acres and the estimated value of all belongings of the school is $100,000. Mrs. Coates' endowment amounted to $20,000 and the college was named in honor of its founder.

The present (1894) President and Trustees are as follows:

TRUSTEES.

Hon. B. E. Rhoades, - - - - - Terre Haute.
Mr. S. C. Stimson, - - - - - - "
" Leslie D. Thomas. - - - - - "
" H. P. Townley, - - - - - - "

PRESIDENT OF THE BOARD.

Mr. H. P. Townley, - - - - - Terre Haute.

The president of the college is the Rev. John Mason Duncan, who is assisted by a large and able faculty.

ST. MARY'S ACADEMIC INSTITUTE.

This is one of the most noted Catholic institutions for the education of young ladies in the West, situated just four miles west of the city in a charming location. It is under the direction of the Sisters of Providence, and it is also the mother house of that order in the United States. The first Academy, a two story brick building, was opened in 1841, in what was then a wilderness, by six Sisters of Providence who emigrated from France. The corner stone of the present large Academy was laid August 15, 1860, by Bishop de St. Palais. The average enrollment now is 200 pupils, coming from a number of Western and Southern states. The Academy celebrated its Golden Jubilee June 23, 1891. The ground of the Institute covers 400 acres, and that part adjacent to the Institute is laid out in a very attractive manner. The imposing stone Chapel, which was begun in 1886, cost $175,000 and is of the Renaissance order. The faculty of the Institute comprises thirty teachers and much attention is given to painting and needle-work. The Academy has its own electric light plant.

CATHOLIC SCHOOLS.

Parochial Schools are attached at present to all the Catholic Schools of Terre Haute except St. Ann's, which church was this year destroyed by fire. St. Joseph's Church has both a male and female school, the estimated value of both being $25,000. The male school is a handsome pressed brick structure. St. Patrick's Church has its male and female School in one large brick building which cost about $8,000. The St. Benedict's (German) Church has a fine Parochial school valued at $20,000. The Sisters of Providence exclusively teach in the Catholic schools of Terre Haute.

CHURCHES.

The Church edifices number forty-two. The various denominations are as follows:

Baptist, 7; Catholic, 4; Christian, 3; Congregational, 3; Evangelical, 2; Jewish Synagogue, 1; Lutheran, 2; Methodist Episcopal, 11; Presbyterian, 3; Protestant Episcopal, 2; Reformed, 2; Seventh Day Advents, 1, and United Brethren, 1.

THE HOME OF THE TROTTER.

Terre Haute is the home of Axtell, the phenomenal.

The Terre Haute race track is famous wherever the trotting horse is known and prized.

The 2:04 track in this city is the fastest in the world. All the greatest horses in America are trained here because the climate, the soil, the grass and the track are the best.

The purses here, $90,000, for a single meeting, are the largest ever offered anywhere.

But these are not the only distinctions for which the city is famous as the center of interest concerning the trotting horse. There are a number of great stock farms here. Very large sums are invested and more is being constantly added in the successful breeding and training of record-beating trotters and high-priced roadsters.

The principal stock farms are as follows:

Warren Park, the home of Axtell, owned by Mr. W. P. Ijams.

Edgewood Stock Farm, the home of Jersey Wilkes, owned by Prest. W. R. McKeen.

Willow Ridge Farm, the property of Mr. P. J. Kaufman.

More Park, owned by Mr. Benj. G. Cox.

Others are Walnut Grove Farm, Beechwood Stock Farm, Anton Mayer Farm, and Jno. Pugh Farm where coach horses are bred.

THE RAILROADS.

There are nine railroads entering Terre Haute. It is on the line of three of the largest railway systems in the country, the Pennsylvania and Vanderbilt systems, and the north and south lines of the Porter system.

The lines are as follows:

Pennsylvania System.	T. H. & I. (Indianapolis Division) 72 miles.
	ST. L. V. & T. H. 168 miles.
	MICHIGAN DIVISION, 223 miles.
	PEORIA " 174 "
Big Four System.	INDIANAPOLIS DIVISION, 75 miles
	ST. LOUIS " 187 "
Porter and "Mackey" Systems.	C. & E. I. 178 miles.
	E. & T. H. 109 "
	E. & I. 138 "

MANUFACTURES AND OTHER BRANCHES OF BUSINESS.

The following table, prepared for the Gazette by Secretary C. M. Thompson, of the Business Men's Association, shows in detail the different branches of business and the number and character of manufactures in 1894.

No. of Establishments.

Agricultural Implements, Machinery, etc	8
Ale, Beer and Mineral Waters	4
Art Specialties	6
Auction Sales	4
Bakers	16
Banks	5
Barrels	7
Baskets, Brooms and Willoware	5
Blacksmiths and Horse Shoers	38
Blank Books, Wood and Paper Boxes	5
Blast Furnace	1
Boilers and Sheet Iron	6
Boots, Shoes, Leather and Leather Goods	68
Books and Stationary	10
Brass Foundries	2
Brick Yards	7
Butchers	10
Candy and Confectioneries	17
Carriages, Wagons and Carts	13
Carpenters and Builders	60
Carpets and House Furnishings	10
Car Works	1
Cigars, Cigarettes and Cheroots	30
Clothing	14
Coal Dealers	20
Coffee, Spice and Flavoring Mills	2
Drugs, Medicines, Paints, Oils, etc	40
Dry Goods and Notions, Wholesale	4
" " " " Retail	15
Dyeing and Bleaching	4
Electric Motors, Heaters, etc	1
Feed and Produce	44
Fish, Produce, etc	3
Flour and Corn Meal	4
Flour Mills	3
Furniture, Awnings and Mattresses	9
Foundries and Machine Shops	3
Gas and Steam Fitting	8
Groceries and Liquors, Wholesale	4
" " " Retail	200
Gunsmiths, Sporting Goods, etc	4
Harness and Saddlery	9
Hardware, Wholesale and Retail	9
Hats and Caps	7
Hominy Mills	3
Hubs and Spokes	1
Ice from River	3
Ice, artificial	2
Iron and Nail Works	1
Iron Manufacturers, Miscellaneous	2
Jewelry	12
Leather and Hides	2
Lime and Cement	5
Locksmiths	2
Marble and Stone Works	7
Millinery	15
Newspapers and Job Printers	10
Optical Instruments	6
Overalls, Pants and Shirts	4
Paper Manufacturers and Dealers	1
Piano Case Works	1
Paper Box Factory	1
Photography	7
Planing Mills	5
Pressed Brick	1
Pumps	3
Queensware	7
Rolling Mills	2
Sash, Blinds, Doors, etc	7
Sewing Machines	3
Shovel, Fork and Ax Works	1
Soap Works	1
Straw Board Mill	1
Stove Foundries	1
Tinware and Plumbing	9
Woolen Mills	1

In the business world Terre Haute enjoys the distinction of having the largest wholesale grocery in the state, Hulman & Co's; the largest wholesale dry goods store, the Havens & Geddes Co. There are many other wholesale houses, nearly every line of goods being represented.

In manufactures the city heads the list with the largest car works in Indiana; two of the largest distilleries in the world; the headquarters and leading plant of the Standard Wheel Co.; the only piano case factory; the only shovel works in Indiana and is the center of overall factories. The next few years will see a great development of the manufacture of paving brick and other clay products in this county. Terre Haute leads all of the cities of the state in flour and hominy milling.

HOTELS.

Until recent years Terre Haute hotels did not rank conspicuously high, but the city is second to none in that respect now. The leading houses are the Terre Haute, which surpasses any in the State, the National, the New Filbeck, the New St. Nicholas, the Melville and the Bronson.

CHARITIES.

The charitable institutions of Terre Haute are in an excellent condition and are successfully accomplishing a great work; the result of a charity that speaks in private and public donations of our citizens and through the munificence of the late Chauncey Rose.

The object of the Society for Organizing Charity is the promotion of whatever tends to the permanent improvement of the poor. S. B. Davis is President of the society and W. C. Smallwood, General Secretary. The society endeavors to make work the basis of relief and to this end runs an employment bureau, a workroom for women and a woodyard for men, where able bodied persons can earn meals and lodging at the Home for the Friendless. Deserving poor, unable to work, are cared for free. Last year the society investigated about 2,500 cases.

St. Anthony's Hospital is now one of the best equipped institutions of its size in the country. It was established in September, 1882, by the Sisters of St. Francis, under whose care it still remains. In 1883 Mr. H. Hulman, its leading benefactor, purchased and fitted up the present building. He was assisted in the enterprise by donations amounting to about $10,000. The new St. Anthony's Hospital was dedicated January 1st, 1884. About 5,000 patients have been cared for with a total mortality from all diseases of about eight per cent. One hundred patients can be accommodated at one time.

The Terre Haute Sanitarium, a pay hospital, is managed by private individuals.

FREE DISPENSARY.

In the will of Chauncey Rose was a provision to set aside $75,000 for the purpose of erecting and maintaining a dispensary for the free distribution of drugs to the poor. The interest has now increased the amount to $130,000. A structure to cost $42,740 is now being built on a $15,000 lot at the corner of Seventh and Cherry streets. This building will furnish a permanent location for the Rose Dispensary, and the rents from the halls, store rooms and offices will increase the annual income. The original sum will be left as a permanent endowment.

THE ROSE HOME AND ST. ANN'S.

The Rose Orphan Home was organized in 1874 and the buildings were formally dedicated on September 3rd, 1884. The permanent endowment fund, the gift of Mr. Rose, consists of investments estimated at $300,000. The buildings, grounds and improvements valued at $113,146, were paid for entirely with interest money. Up to the present date 463 children have been taken into the home. The average number is 90. L. P. Alden is the Superintendent.

St. Ann's Orphan Asylum, located at the south east corner of Thirteenth Street and Sixth Avenue, is connected with St. Ann's church and is under the direction of the Sisters of Providence. Girls, only, are cared for here.

OLD LADIES' HOME.

The Old Ladies' Home, which is located on north Fifth Street, has, during the six years of its existence, furnished a friendly shelter to many feeble and needy women. W. R. McKeen purchased the site for this purpose and turned the management over to the Rose Ladies' Aid Society. The maintenance is by voluntary contributions and small legacies, which have been left it.

A list of Terre Haute's charitable institutions would be incomplete without mention of the Rose Ladies' Aid Society, Hebrew Ladies' Aid Society, Woman's Christian Temperance Uuion. Woman's Relief Corps, and the Aid Societies in the various churches, which devote much time to alleviating the wants of the poor.

NEWSPAPERS AND MAGAZINES.

The newspapers now in Terre Haute (1894) were most of them established many years ago. The fact that during the past twenty years nearly twenty daily papers, started in competition with those below named, have suspended, with disastrous financial loss, would seem to indicate that the city will not support a larger number.

NEWSPAPERS.

The Daily Evening and Weekly Gazette (1868), published by Wm. C. and Spencer F. Ball; the Daily Morning and Weekly Express (1821), by Geo. M. Allen; the Saturday Evening Mail (1870), by Messrs. A. C. Duddleston and Fred Piepenbrink; the Daily Evening and Weekly Journal (1884) by Jacob E. Wollf; the Afro-American Journal (1890), by J. W. Washington; the Wabash Exponent (1891) by J. W. Jarvis.

MAGAZINES.

Locomotive Firemen's Magazine (1875), National organ of the B. of L. F.; the Military Mirror (1893), by Geo. W. Biegler and O. Hippelhauser.

TERRE HAUTE BUSINESS MEN'S ASSOCIATION.

The Terre Haute Business Men's Association has for officers (1894), Herman Hulman, President; C. M. Thompson, Secretary; Frank McKeen, Treasurer. The rooms of the association are at 631½ Wabash Ave. The chief object of the association is to encourage manufactures.

MISCELLANEOUS NOTES.

Terre Haute has the cheapest artificial fuel gas in Indiana; also the cheapest steam coal.

The electric street railway system has no superior.

There are many miles of modern street paving.

The Union Station is the handsomest in Indiana outside of Indianapolis.

There are two artesian wells of the highest medicinal value; also large and well appointed bath houses.

The soil in this section has no superior in the world for the production of vegetables and cereals.

HON. RICHARD W. THOMPSON.

PHOTO BY BIEL.

SENATOR DANIEL W. VOORHEES.

WM R. McKEEN,

President Vandalia Ry.

HERMAN HULMAN, ESQ.

FROM PHOTO BY BIEL.

HON. THOMAS H. NELSON,

Ex. U. S. Minister to Chili; U. S. Envoy to Mexico, etc.

ROM PHOTO BY BIEL.

WM. E. McLEAN,

Attorney, Ex-Deputy U. S. Commissioner of Pensions.

FROM PHOTO BY BIEL.

BLACKFORD CONDIT, D. D.

Retired Presbyterian Minister.

REV. J. H. CRUM, D. D.,
Pastor First Congregational Church,

REV. S. V. LEECH, D. D.

Pastor Centenary M. E. Church.

REV. J. S. HOLMES, D. D.

Pastor First Baptist Church.

FROM PHOTO BY BIEL.

REV. R. V. HUNTER, Pastor.

Central Presbyterian Church.

PHOTO BY BIEL.

REV. FRANK A. MORGAN,

Pastor Central Christian Church.

REV. J. L. HOAGLAND,

Associate Pastor Centenary M. E. Church.

REV. JNO. RYVES,

Rector of St. Ann's.

WILLIAM W. PARSONS,

President Indiana State Normal School.

History and Philosophy of Education.

FROM PHOTO BY BIEL.

HOWARD SANDISON,

Vice-President Indiana State Normal School, Mental Science and Methods.

PHOTO BY BIEL.

ROBERT G. GILLUM,

Indiana State Normal School, Physics and Chemistry.

FROM PHOTO BY BIEL.

LOUIS J. RETTGER,

Indiana State Normal School, Biology.

FROM PHOTO BY BIEL.

FRANCIS M. STALKER,

Indiana State Normal School, Psychology and Methods.

PHOTO BY BIEL.

JAMES B. WISELY,

Indiana State Normal School, Grammar, Rhetoric and Composition.

CHARLES M. CURRY,

Indiana State Normal School, Assistant in Reading and Literature.

ARTHUR CUNNINGHAM,

Indiana State Normal School, Librarian.

FROM PHOTO BY BIEL.

WM. H. WILEY,

Superintendent Public Schools.

FROM PHOTO BY BIEL.

H. W. CURRY,

Superintendent Vigo County Schools

VIGO COUNTY COURT HOUSE.

DAVID N. TAYLOR,

Judge 43rd. Judicial Circuit of Indiana.

FROM PHOTO BY BIEL.

HUGH D. ROQUET,

Democratic Candidate for County Clerk.

FROM PHOTO BY BIEL.

J. W. STOUT,

Sheriff of Vigo County.

FROM PHOTO BY BIEL.

GEO. A. SCHAAL,

Auditor Vigo County.

FROM PHOTO BY BIEL.

JOHN L. WALSH,

County Treasurer.

FROM PHOTO BY BIEL.

LEVI G. HUGHES,

Recorder Vigo County.

FROM PHOTO BY BIEL.

Dr. W. R. MATTOX,

County Coroner.

FROM PHOTO BY BIEL.

CHAS. W. HOFF,

County Assessor, Vigo County.

FROM PHOTO BY BIEL.

JOHN BEAL,

President Board County Commissioners.

FROM PHOTO BY BIEL.

JOHN McFALL,

County Commissioner.

PHOTO BY BIEL.

RALPH H. SPARKS,

Surveyor of Vigo County.

FROM PHOTO BY BIEL.

FRED A ROSS,

Mayor of Terre Haute.

W. W. HAUCK,

City Treasurer.

CHARLES BALCH,

City Treasurer, Elect.

CHAS. H. GOODWIN,

City Clerk.

FROM PHOTO BY BIEL.

PETER M. FOLEY,

City Attorney.

FROM PHOTO BY BIEL.

C. MEAGHER,

Sup't Police.

FROM PHOTO BY BIEL.

H. S. BOSLER,

City Engineer.

FROM PHOTO BY BIEL.

MICHAEL J. O'CONNELL,

Assessor Harrison Tp.

FROM PHOTO BY BIEL.

GEO. W. FARIS,

Attorney, Republican Nominee for Congress.

SAM. R. HAMILL,

Attorney at Law.

FROM PHOTO BY BIEL.

D. W. HENRY,

Attorney at Law.

FROM PHOTO BY BIEL.

ROBERT B. STIMSON,

Attorney, Stimson, Stimson & Higgins.

FROM PHOTO BY BIEL.

SAMUEL C. STIMSON,

Attorney, Stimson, Stimson & Higgins.

GEORGE E PUGH,

Attorney.

FROM PHOTO BY BIEL.

SAMUEL M. HUSTON,

Attorney at Law. Republican Candidate for Prosecuting Attorney.

FORM PHOTO BY BIEL.

E. H. REDMAN.

Attorney.

FROM PHOTO BY BIEL.

ALVIN M. HIGGINS,

Attorney, Stimson, Stimson & Higgins,

H. A. CONDIT,

Attorney, of Stimson, Stimson & Higgins,

FROM PHOTO BY BIEL.

W. H. TABER,

Attorney at Law.

FROM PHOTO BY BIEL.

A. W. SPAIN, M. D.

President County Board of Health.

FROM PHOTO BY BEIL.

WILBUR O. JENKINS, M. D.

President of City Board of Health.

LE'ON J. WILLIEN, M. D.

JNO. R. CRAPO, M. D.

FROM PHOTO BY BIEL.

F. W. SHALEY, M. D.

FROM PHOTO BY BIEL.

ALLEN H. DONHAM,

Postmaster.

FROM PHOTO BY BIEL.

WM. O. PATTON,

Assistant Postmaster.

B. G. HUDNUT,

President Vigo County National Bank,

also President of the Hudnut Company.

GEORGE E. FARRINGTON,

Secretary & General Agent Vandalia Line.

N. K. ELLIOTT,

General Superintendent Vandalia Line.

C. R. PEDDLE,

Purchasing Agent Vandalia Line.

FROM PHOTO BY BIEL.

R. D. DIGGES,

Ticket Agent Union Depot, Vandalia Line.

A. G. NICHOSON,

Central States Dispatch, Fast Freight.

FROM PHOTO BY BIEL.

FRANK E. BENJAMIN,

Agent American Express Co.

FROM PHOTO BY BIEL.

LYMAN P. ALDEN,

Sup't Rose Orphan Home.

FROM PHOTO BY BIEL.

J. BREINIG,

Leader Ringgold Band and Orchestra.

Late Leader 24th and 91st Ind. Vol. Band.

FROM PHOTO BY BIEL.

C. H. PAYNE,

Manager The Hughes Decorating Co.

FROM PHOTO BY BIEL.

W. C. SMALLWOOD,

General Secretary Organized Charities.

FROM PHOTO BY BIEL.

W. H. FLOYD,

Architect of Floyd & Stone.

FROM PHOTO BY BIEL.

GUY STONE,

Floyd & Stone, Architects.

FROM PHOTO BY BIEL.

JOHN A. BOGGS,

With Jos. Strong & Co.

FROM PHOTO BY BIEL.

JAS. C. COUPER,

Manager Standard Wheel Co's Factory.

FROM PHOTO BY BIEL.

LOUIS P. SEEBURGER,

Democratic Candidate for Sheriff.

FROM PHOTO BY BIEL.

J. W. LANDRUM,

Manager Terre Haute Coal and Lime Co., and
Secretary Coal Bluff Mining Co.

FROM PHOTO BY BIEL.

WILLIS WRIGHT,

Furniture, Carpets and Drapery.

FROM PHOTO BY BIEL.

E. L. NORCROSS,

Manager Western Union Telegraph Co.

FROM PHOTO BY BIEL.

T. J. GRIFFITH,

Palace Shoe Store.

FROM PHOTO BY BIEL.

JAMES A. NISBET,

Undertaker.

FROM PHOTO BY BIEL.

W. M. SLAUGHTER,

Real Estate Broker, Loan and Insurance.

FROM PHOTO BY BIEL.

JOHN FOULKES,

Real Estate, Loan and Insurance Agent.

FROM PHOTO BY BIEL.

H. T. BIEL,

Photographer.

FROM PHOTO BY BIEL.

CHAS. E. GAREN,

New Method Laundry.

FROM PHOTO BY BIEL.

WM. A. HUNTER,

Hunter's Livery, Ball Bearing Harness.

FROM PHOTO BY BIEL.

C. W. KELLY,

Mining, Municipal and General Eng.

FROM PHOTO BY BIEL.

JAMES M. DISHON,

Bill Paster and Distributor.

FROM PHOTO BY BIEL.

GEO. H. GREENMAN,

Manager Pixley & Co., Clothiers and Furnishers.

FROM PHOTO BY BIEL.

GEO. R. GRIMES,

Civil Engineer and Contractor.

FROM PHOTO BY BIEL.

JAMES E. SOMES,

Pharmacist.

FROM PHOTO BY BIEL.

C. E. ERVIN,

Dentist.

FROM PHOTO BY BIEL.

DR. C. F. WILLIAMS,

Dentist.

FROM PH⌐ O BY BIEL'

C. M. THOMPSON,

Secretary Terre Haute Business Men's Association.

FROM PHOTO BY BIEL.

W. C. ISBELL,

President Terre Haute Commercial College.

FROM PHOTO BY BIEL.

The Old Reliable TERRE HAUTE COMMERCIAL COLLEGE, Established in 1862.

FROM PHOTO BY BIEL.

HENRY P. TOWNLEY, ESQ.,

President of the Board of Trustees of Coates College.

FORM PHOTO BY BIEL.

THE REV. JOHN MASON DUNCAN,

President of Coates College.

COATES COLLEGE, Looking South-East in May.

FROM PHOTO BY BIEL.

A COATES COLLEGE GREEK GROUP.

FROM PHOTO BY BIEL.

THE COATES COLLEGE GYMNASIUM

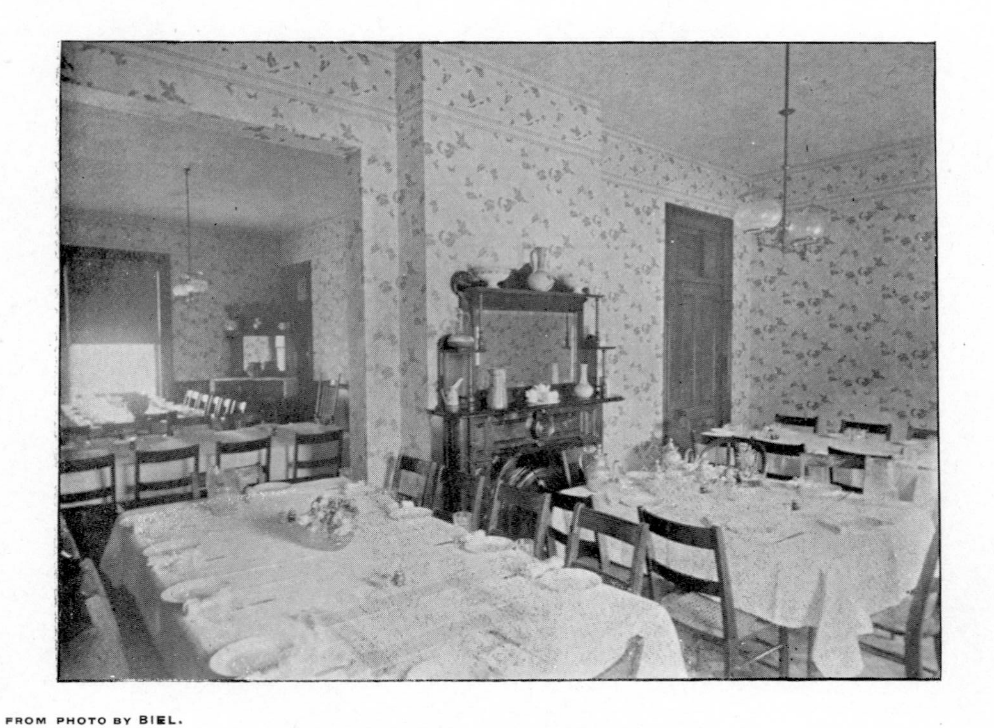

FROM PHOTO BY BIEL.

Two of the COATES COLLEGE Dining Rooms

FROM PHOTO BY BIEL.

KENILWORTH TENNIS COURT, at Coates College.

CHARLES BAUR, Proprietor

TERRE HAUTE HOUSE.

FROM PHOTO BY BIEL. FLOYD & STONE, ARCHITECTS.

THE NEW FILBECK.

FROM PHOTO BY BIEL.

ST. NICHOLAS HOTEL, Maurice Walsh, Proprietor.

FORM PHOTO BY BIEL.

GRAND STAND at the Great 2.04 Terre Haute Track.

FROM PHOTO BY BIEL.

ROSE ORPHAN HOME.

FROM PHOTO BY BIEL.

Residence of WM. R. McKEEN.

FROM PHOTO BY BIEL.

Residence of N. K. ELLIOTT.

FROM PHOTO BY BIEL.

Residence of B. G. HUDNUT.

ST. ANTHONY'S HOSPITAL.

JOS. STRONG BLOCK.

FORM PHOTO BY BIEL.

NORTHERN ROLLING MILLS.
WABASH DISTILLERY.

FROM PHOTO BY BIEL.

HOSE CO. NO. 4. CHEMICAL ENGINE NO. 1

of Terre Haute Fire Department.

FROM PHOTO BY BIEL.

UNION PASSENGER DEPOT.

FROM PHOTO BY BIEL.

HULMAN & COMPANY,

Wholesale Grocers.

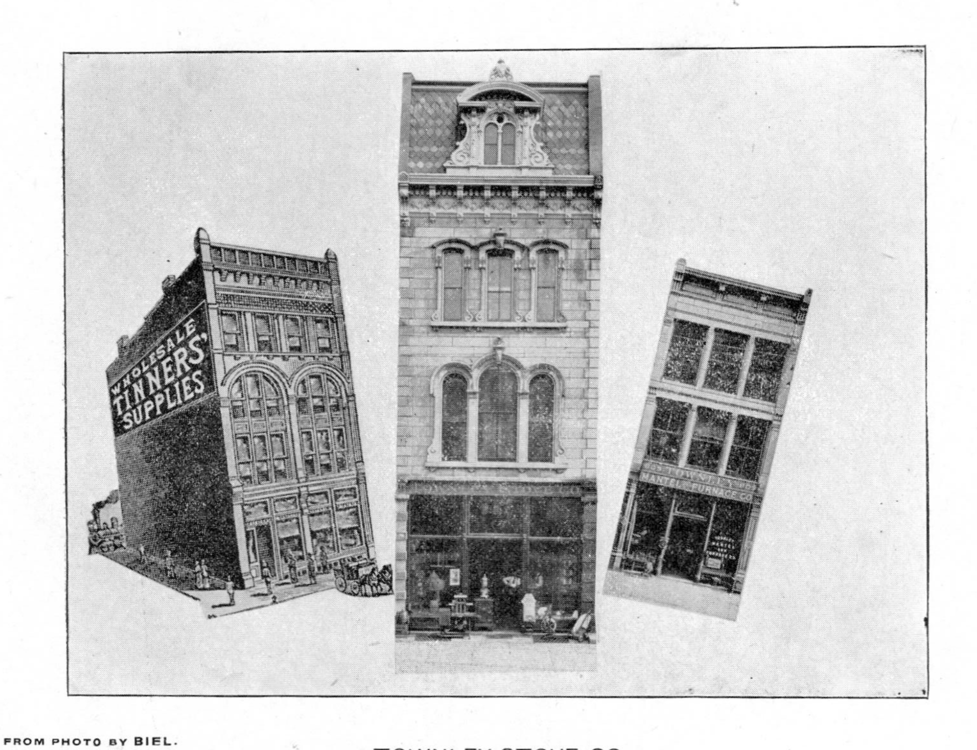

FROM PHOTO BY BIEL.

TOWNLEY STOVE CO.

Branches: { Townley Metal Co., Kansas City, Mo.
Townley Mantel and Furnace Co., Terre Haute, Ind.

FROM PHOTO BY BIEL.

ELLIOTT & SMITH, Wholesale Hat House.

FROM PHOTO BY BIEL.

NATIONAL STATE BANK.

FROM PHOTO BY BIEL.

BREINIG FLATS, Property of H. L. Breinig, Carpets, Furniture and Stoves.

FROM PHOTO BY BIEL.

EXCHANGE ARTESIAN MINERAL SPRINGS, BATH HOUSE.

FROM PHOTO BY BIEL.

GOVERNMENT BUILDING.

FROM PHOTO BY BIEL.

Washington Ave. PRESBYTERIAN CHURCH.

FROM PHOTO BY BIEL.

NEW ASBURY CHURCH

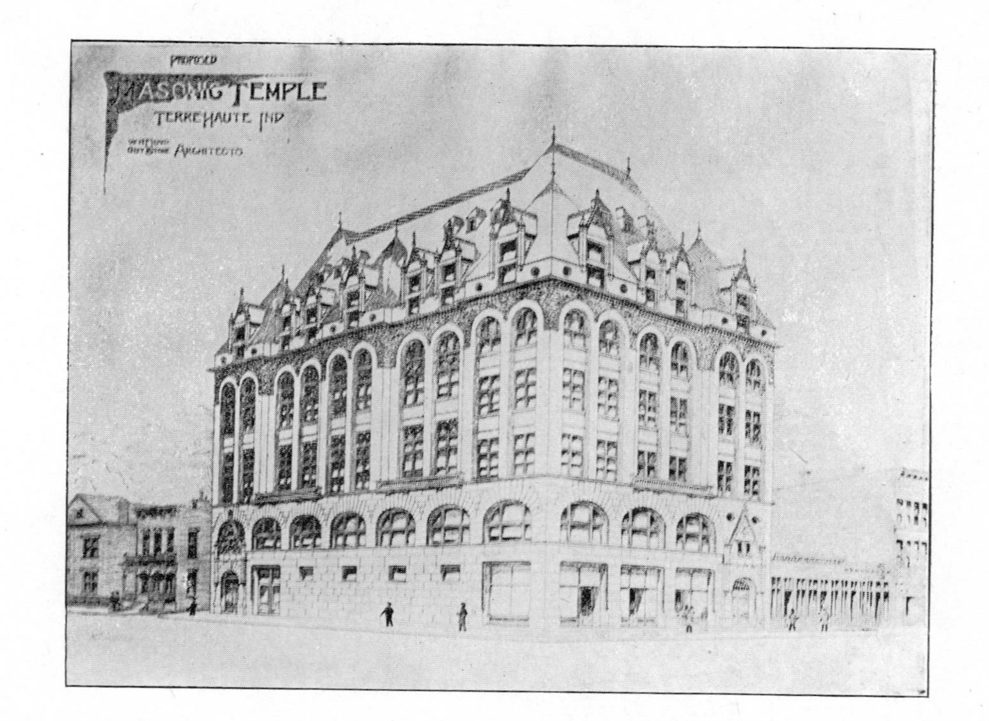

FROM PHOTO BY BIEL.

FLOYD & STONE, ARCHITECTS.

PROPOSED MASONIC TEMPLE

FROM PHOTO BY BIEL.

INDIANA STATE NORMAL SCHOOL.

FROM PHOTO BY BIEL.

TERRE HAUTE HIGH SCHOOL.

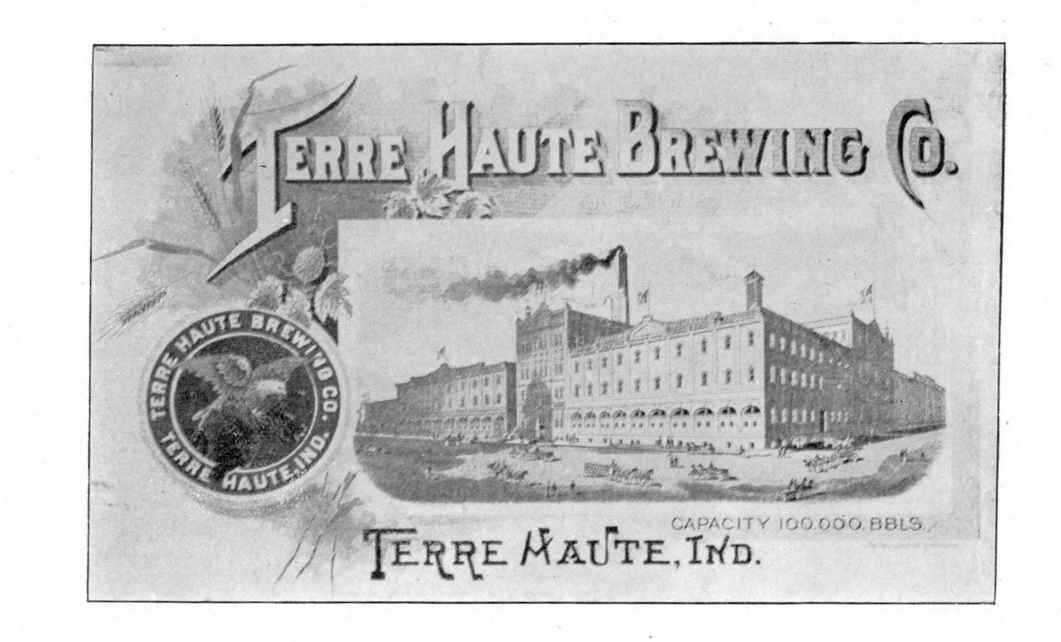
TERRE HAUTE BREWING CO.
TERRE HAUTE BREWING CO. TERRE HAUTE, IND.
CAPACITY 100,000 BBLS.
TERRE HAUTE, IND.

FROM PHOTO BY BIEL.

CHAPEL at HIGHLAND LAWN CEMETERY,

FROM PHOTO BY BIEL.

VIEW AT HIGHLAND LAWN CEMETERY.

FROM PHOTO BY BIEL.

View from top of Court House looking East.

FROM PHOTO BY BIEL.

View from top of Court House looking North.

FROM PHOTO BY BIEL.

Looking East on Wabash Avenue from Third Street.

FROM PHOTO BY BIEL.

Looking North on South Sixth Street from Col. Thompson's Residence.

FROM PHOTO BY BIEL.

Looking South of Seventh Street from College Street.

FROM PHOTO BY BIEL.

VIEW IN FOREST PARK.

FROM PHOTO BY BIEL.

WATER VIEW IN FORBEST PARK.